LESSON FOR THE HOMELESS

I understand they stare but don't worry you can still blind them with your inner light. I know sometimes it will get cold, but you must keep a warm smile. When you start your day—pray. There may be times in your life that seem dark but allow your mind to be your sunlight. You can make it! Leave that box, leave that staircase, and leave that garbage bin! Push upward because there's nowhere else to go, but up! If they laugh at you have a conversation with them. Ask if they are homeless inside their hearts. Ask how you can get to where they are. The greatest gift is knowing how to get what you need. This is called learning to fish. Once you learn you will always have "more homes" rather than homes "less".

BLESSING: Your location is NOT you destination.

D0166650

YOUR MOTIVATION

_____

_____

_____

_____

_____

_____

_____

_____

_____

_____

_____

_____

_____

_____

_____

_____

_____

_____

_____

_____

_____

_____

LESSON FOR THE FRIENDSHIP

Friendship is a bond you must always invest in. The lessons you learn from friendship are indescribable. The best teacher for this is experience. Now don't get me wrong, you will lose many friends, gain enough, struggle with some and grow into something beyond friendship with few. Life will place individuals in your path for assistance to your destination. But one must remember, not everyone is worthy of the title 'Friend'. Friendship is a commitment between neutral spirits that serve to elevate one another to higher plateaus.

Have you had a friend? I mean a true homie? One who is always there even when they are not physically there? One who keeps it real and doesn't force a friendship but allows it to manifest naturally? Friendships will have their ups and downs but you must always remember the law of friendships. They are extended family due to commitment. We all need them because they are investments that enhance our soul. Without them you will have more lonely walks than most.

BLESSING: May your true friend be your H.O.M.I.E.: Heavens Only Model In Everlasting-friendship.

YOUR MOTIVATION

LESSON ON YOUR PATH

The path on which you walk was made just for you. Everything was made perfect to cross your path. You will make mistakes, you will reach dead ends and you will even make wrong turns during your travels. But you must remember each situation was made perfect to help you reach your destination. Embrace all your experiences as lessons because they will be the fuel that keeps you going. You will get flats; need personal oil changes and mental tune-ups, so be prepared. Sometimes your path will lead to surprises but keep your Triple-A card of persistence and all will be well. You will travel your path alone most of the time, but once in a while there will be someone in the passenger side. Remember, their destination isn't the same as yours. Your destination was designed just for you! So walk, strut, run, jog or speed down your path because you only travel it once.

BLESSING: Move in divine order. Live in blessings.
Eat in peace.

YOUR MOTIVATION

LESSON FOR THE COLLEGE STUDENT

My Dear College Student,

You are in a position that many yearn for. You are in a position that people take for granted. But I know people don't understand what you've gone through to get where you are. They don't know you are the first in your family to attend College. They don't know school became an escape from the abuse you once endured. I know and understand the title you bear and it will all be okay in the end. I know you studied as much as you could for that test, but it was still difficult to pass. I know finding out your pregnant is hard but stay focused. You can be strong where you are. You are learning, you are growing and people are praying for you. Don't give up or give in to those who tell you different. You need to be that doctor because there will be a child who needs you. There will be someone wrongfully accused who needs a strong lawyer. Keep yourself safe and study smart! There is nothing to hold you down. It is false evidence. Do not feed into it. You are great, highly recognized and highly favored. If someone tells you differently...graduate with a degree.

BLESSING: May your college years enhance your student activities on the campus of Life University.

YOUR MOTIVATION

LESSON ON RELATIONSHIP/ PARTNERSHIP

Let me ask you a question. Why do you waste your time on an individual that shows you no love or affection? Why would you protect someone who wouldn't do it for you? There should not be tears of sadness in your eyes. I know you have issues—we all have issues. However, if you are in a relationship it becomes a partnership; meaning you work together for a common goal. I'm not saying it will be easy but there must be a balance. One cannot be out all night while the other constantly takes care of home—that is not balance.

Let me school you on something. Relationship means to relate. If the both of you are not relating then there is no balance. If you're in an unbalanced relationship, issues will always arise that cannot be solved due to lack of connection. If you believe this is a lesson that speaks directly to you, you already know what needs to be done.

BLESSING: May you begin to solve your personal issues before going into a relationship, which may bring forth new issues.

YOUR MOTIVATION

LESSON FOR THOSE WHO DOUBT

Never doubt a person who has never had anything he/ she wanted in life. Never belittle an individual for life may see fit to place you in their shoes. For instance, many people believe homeless individuals lack the mind capacity to get into a home. They are wrong! If you believe a degree is the measurement for intelligence, you must have never heard of self-made millionaires who have never touched a college classroom.

Those who doubt never had someone invest in their own dreams. Those who don't believe don't dream, and if you don't dream—you are not living. So if you ever doubt someone you can do one of two things: apologize and try to help the individual or watch them rise to become more than you.

BLESSING: May you never doubt because if you doubt another, you will doubt yourself.

YOUR MOTIVATION

LESSON FOR THE SINGLE PARENT

Dear Single Parent,

First let me say how proud I am of you for doing what people thought could not be done—taking care of children by yourself. I am proud of you. Remember that each one of your children will tell you the same when they realize you are the reason they made it. What doesn't kill you always makes you stronger.

I know that you cry when no one is around. I know you're trying to figure out how to keep your job when you can't find a sitter, but don't worry. I know you want to go back to school, but learn from where you are and from what you've been through. You are strength and motivation for each day you look at the struggle and say, "I am going to make it." You have already made it and will continue to make it. Dear parent, you are loved.

BLESSING: May you know that there is no one like you . . . NO ONE! You are highly loved and respected.

YOUR MOTIVATION

LESSON ON GREATNESS

Straight and to the point: to achieve greatness you must do more than the normal, average and minimum amount. There is nothing easy about achieving this title. It takes the maximum amount of time and energy mixed with the power to focus. One must endure pain, struggle and sadness while balancing it with smiles and laughter, because once you achieve "greatness" you may still feel or be average. It is maintaining the title that will show greatness. When you achieve and focus on maintaining this, you will endure more than most people. Greatness takes personal sacrifice, discipline and dedication to a level few can withstand. To begin, focus on one thing at a time. It is better to put all your energy in a certain area, than to put some energy in all areas. This way you won't regret putting more time in a situation because you would have already done the best you could with the time you had. Greatness: It is like achieving royalty.

BLESSING: Greatness is the proper way of describing what most individuals don't do.

YOUR MOTIVATION

LESSON ON MISSING A GOOD THING

Missing a good thing is a regret that may affect individuals, couples and even countries. Lets take people for example. People breakup friendships and love relationships because they don't think its worth anything. However, once the person who's seemingly worthless begins to flourish without the other, regret seeps in and becomes self-doubt regarding the choice made. There are people who were born just to spread love in the hearts of others, but the supposed recipient may not know how to treat or embrace that love. When it is real and genuine—love is missed. It becomes something sought out but not found. The reason being real, genuine love isn't the same in everyone.

Missing a good thing will be shown through excessive text messaging, staring or conversations full of apologies. You know missing a good thing is not a good thing . . . especially when you know it will never come back.

BLESSING: May you appreciate all that you receive in life and invest what's necessary to keep a good thing and make it great.

YOUR MOTIVATION

LESSON ON WEALTH

Wealth is the formation of words expressed in books and by individuals that show others how to produce positive results. Most people believe that monetary figures are the definition of "wealth". Do not believe that! You accumulate financial wealth by applying the knowledge you gain. The more you learn the more wealth you accumulate in the mind, body and soul. An individual, who has no wealth in knowledge and lots of money, is only rich—but an individual who has an abundance of knowledge is or will become wealthy.

BLESSING: May you realize that wealth is not determined by the amount of money in your account, but by the amount of knowledge you retain and put into practice.

YOUR MOTIVATION

LESSON ON FAITH

Faith is a powerful tool when it comes to you and what you decide to pursue. Many people claim that they have faith and it is always put to the test. As you wake up daily, always remember that faith is an invisible force like air for your spirit. When you are on your last dime, when you lose a loved one and when people don't believe in you—you must keep the faith. It shows spiritual and individual strength from the soul.

No matter what the situation is, you must keep the faith. As long as you keep the faith there will always be another chance. There will always be another opportunity. When others say no, you say YES! When others say doubt, you must (with complete confidence) believe!

BLESSING: May your faith doctor your inner being when you are hurt. Your faith is GOD's air blown from heaven.

YOUR MOTIVATION

LESSON ON THE STAGE OF LIFE

Everyday we perform on the stage of life. Each moment is photographed by people you call friends. Your audience is in heaven looking down, cheering you on as you play the lead role. You must embrace this time because it could be your final debut. So, perform each day as if it's the grand finale.

You want more...

Your day is the stage.
Your name is the movie title.
Your experiences are your acting coaches.
Your enemies are your real critics.
Your performance is your legacy.

BLESSING: Lets just say there are too many to talk about.

YOUR MOTIVATION

_____

_____

_____

_____

_____

_____

_____

_____

_____

_____

_____

_____

_____

_____

_____

_____

_____

_____

_____

_____

_____

_____

LESSON ON PERSONAL LOSS

You must learn the lesson of a person's value in your life. Everyone needs to understand that our time on this earth is limited. So whenever you have a chance, express your love to someone. There is nothing more hurtful and depressing than to be unable to tell someone that you appreciate him or her when they are here. People come into our lives for reasons and seasons. Some will live and never see you again; some may pass away and you will never see them again. So, while they are here enjoy each other's presence—laugh, talk and grow together. It is only then that people live on through your memories and experiences. Don't live with the regret of not saying what your heart wants to express.

BLESSING: Even though you lose someone in the physical world, you gain an angel in the spiritual world. LIVE LIFE!

YOUR MOTIVATION

_____

_____

_____

_____

_____

_____

_____

_____

_____

_____

_____

_____

_____

_____

_____

_____

_____

_____

_____

_____

_____

LESSON ON UNDERSTANDING

This is for those who need to understand the life of great Kings. Today's great Kings are having a rough time with their royal family. Some of them aren't living up to their name, so the great Kings are struggling to rise without the push they need from Kings and Queens that have come before.

My great Kings: Rise high and claim the thrown that is yours. Never be afraid to live the life of royalty. Greatness is in your blood. Show power in your stance; show strength in your leadership; show compassion and love to those who help you achieve greatness. You are more than they say you are. Build your kingdom on faith and expand your empire with order. Blessed is the child who has his own.

BLESSING: May you rise tall and strong to show that you are here for something.

YOUR MOTIVATION

LESSON ON KICKING ROCKS

This lesson is about keeping your youth alive. As you get older you must remember that doing things with a youthful spirit helps you enjoy life constantly. You are what you think! "Kick rocks" is a term you should use when you're frustrated or in a state of mind that you don't like. Tell yourself to kick rocks and keep it moving. Don't waste your time on old things when there are so many new things to do and create. Always enjoy your youth, creativity and the beauty in life. If someone tries to take that freedom from you—just tell him or her to kick rocks and keep it moving.

BLESSING: May each day bring the youthful surprise of new joy and happiness.

YOUR MOTIVATION

_____

_____

_____

_____

_____

_____

_____

_____

_____

_____

_____

_____

_____

_____

_____

_____

_____

_____

_____

_____

_____

_____

LESSON FROM THEN TO NOW

From now on remember where you have come from. Look at where you are now, because "then" is the past. You cannot change it, but you can make up for it. People may not know your pain and happiness from then, so now is the time to open up. You can shine no matter where you are now or where you were then. From then to now...

BLESSING: What you do now is the after effect of what you have done then.

YOUR MOTIVATION

_____

_____

_____

_____

_____

_____

_____

_____

_____

_____

_____

_____

_____

_____

_____

_____

_____

_____

_____

_____

_____

_____

LESSON ON BEING IDEAL

To be ideal one must commit to being different. One must embrace the concept of being more than average. When you choose to be ideal, you are telling the world there is no one like you. So, you must project it in your appearance, your thinking, your communication and your overall image. Being ideal is a continuous process, because there will always be a part of your life that needs detoxifying. It could be your character or your conversation; no matter what it is, it will have to change. Ideal people are recognized as quality beings that possess value in the world. Claim within yourself that ideal is who you are with a foundation of greatness.

BLESSING: Practice perfection in all situations, because when you perfect your practice you will get ideal results

YOUR MOTIVATION

LESSON ON FINDING YOURSELF

Finding out who you are is an everyday search. For as long as you live you will continue to learn something new about yourself. Once you learn something about you, you begin to grow. The most important thing is to be genuine in your search. At times people fake it 'til they make it, but you must be yourself at all times. Your search will be a rollercoaster, but it is a ride that everyone should want to experience. Don't be afraid of the height of success you get or the speed at which you get it, because every moment is perfect as it is. Find yourself and you will free yourself.

BLESSING: May you look through your heart's eye and understand why people love you just for being you.

YOUR MOTIVATION

_____

_____

_____

_____

_____

_____

_____

_____

_____

_____

_____

_____

_____

_____

_____

_____

_____

_____

_____

LESSON ON COMPLICATIONS

Things are never as complicated as they seem. When you try to force what should come easy things then become complicated. People swim underwater everyday thinking they're unable to come up for air–drowning in their struggles. We must all understand that we will all have our time to shine, so we should pace ourselves and swim with ease.

Things are never as complicated as they seem. Don't get me wrong we all encounter tidal waves, but when we embrace the flow instead of resisting it, we come out on top without complication. People—don't make this day complicated! Just come up for air whenever you finish a lap.

BLESSING: Don't complicate your day with negative currents; move towards your goals with waves of positivity.

YOUR MOTIVATION

_____

_____

_____

_____

_____

_____

_____

_____

_____

_____

_____

_____

_____

_____

_____

_____

_____

_____

_____

_____

_____

_____

LESSON ON SUCCESS

Success is a responsibility that one must prepare for. People fall short because of fear or lack of preparation. When you achieve success there will be a distinction between yourself and others. Are you prepared to stand out? When you reach your peak there will be love lost, friendships broken and shifting points of view. You must be prepared to accept the positive and negative effects. Success comes in different levels so people will receive it in different ways, but the effects will always be the same. When you become successful remember to change for the better even if others change for the worse. You must stay grounded at all times because you will be tempted and tested. You will receive mountains of attention, but remain humble and learn from your mistakes. This will keep your foundation strong and give longevity to your success. Also remember that success is not forced, it is embraced. It is determined by the results of your actions.

BLESSING: Success is the product of how you build your environment.

YOUR MOTIVATION

LESSON ON LOVE

Love is the lyric that your heart writes when your emotions cannot speak. We fall in love with many things that give us reason to live. Have you ever fallen in love? I'm talking so in love with music that you dance with it in the mirror. Have you ever fallen so in love with a person as soon as they're out of sight you miss them? Love cannot be explained because it has many faces. It is the only real freedom of expression. People are only great at something when they LOVE what they do. To be self-confident, happy, successful and great—you must first love your self.

BLESSING: Love is best described as a drink that evokes the feeling of all four seasons in a cup of paradise.

YOUR MOTIVATION

LESSON ON DREAMS

Dreams are what keep people living. Everyone has a dream, and everyone's dream is made just for him or her. So, it is okay if others don't believe in your dream. Remember this on the way to making it a reality. As you dream, remember that it is the caterpillar of your hearts desire. We must be molded, transformed and ready to embrace it as the butterfly of our reality.

BLESSING: May your dreams be the color in your rainbow so you can be an example of beauty after a storm

YOUR MOTIVATION

_____

_____

_____

_____

_____

_____

_____

_____

_____

_____

_____

_____

_____

_____

_____

_____

_____

_____

_____

_____

LESSON ON TODAY

Today is the result of what you did yesterday. You cannot change yesterday, but you can reflect upon it for understanding of today. Today will be tomorrow's yesterday. So, what you do at this present moment is an investment for your next today. Your return can be a positive or a negative; it all depends on you. Today is the writing that becomes permanent ink in your history tomorrow. What ever you want out of life start on it today. It doesn't matter if it's a minute, hour or the entire day. Its best that you start today, because just like tomorrow, today was not promised.

BLESSING: May today feel like a cup of love sipped in the backyard of Spring.

YOUR MOTIVATION

LESSON ON BEING UNBREAKABLE

You will not fold, give in or be stopped! To be unbreakable you must have a spirit as strong as leather and a heart as solid as a rock. Weak words will not move you. Your success is written on the wall of longevity and no one will live long enough to break it down. Unbreakable is what you are. It is why your enemies are mad. There is no measure for you because you come from a long line of unbreakable people. Where you stand today cannot and will not be moved!! Go hard in all that you do and know that you are one of a kind. You won't be moved no matter what!

BLESSING: Unbreakable is the definition of a person who moves mountains of naysayers and stands on the clouds of achievement.

YOUR MOTIVATION

LESSON ON BEING HAPPY

Just do what you feel is right in your heart and live the way you want. At the end of the day only you have to live and sleep with your decisions. Some individuals believe others can determine what makes them happy—not so. It's as simple as writing your name...Do what makes you smile everyday no matter what and trust in what you believe and say.

BLESSING: Remember only you can paint your perfect picture in an imperfect world. Others have to deal with being imperfect in their own world.

YOUR MOTIVATION

_____

_____

_____

_____

_____

_____

_____

_____

_____

_____

_____

_____

_____

_____

_____

_____

_____

_____

_____

_____

LESSON ON KNOWING YOUR HEAVEN

In the morning you can lay next to heaven or you can be in the midst of an invisible emptiness you mistake for love. At times we take for granted what we have in life and allow ourselves to make love to something or someone who doesn't love us in return. If this is you, don't worry because your heaven will be revealed in time. Believe it will happen but don't attach a timeline to it. Heaven will reveal itself in the form of your other half to make you whole. When this happens you will never be the same because you will always remember what it was like not to wake up next to heaven, and you won't allow it to happen again.

BLESSING: May your clouds help you reach the level of your heaven.

YOUR MOTIVATION

LESSON ON BEING YOURSELF

This is one lesson that many people struggle with. Being yourself is a must in order to achieve success. When you are yourself it allows people to know and understand the true you. It also allows you to recognize what people honestly think of you. When you lose sight of being yourself, you miss gifts and opportunities meant just for you. Why be phony when you can keep it real? If you want an honest opinion—be honest with yourself. When people know you for who you really are they give you more respect. If you ever have the urge to be something other than yourself, remember this quote: "It is better to be hated for being who you truly are than to be loved for being someone you're not."

BLESSING: Being yourself allows you to be the main character in the motion picture of life.

YOUR MOTIVATION

LESSON ON REFLECTIONS

Reflection is not just what you see in the mirror, it is also what you get back after putting things into the universe. Some people call it karma, but I call it reflect of actions. Some people don't like to look at their reflection because they are disappointed in what they see. For example if you tell someone they treat people wrong and the individual says, "I'm sorry," they are actually saying sorry to what is being reflected to them. If you do everything with love and are confident in what you speak, there is no reason to be sorry. Being or saying sorry is another way of putting your head down. You must reflect the highest form of positive action for you are the reflection of your inner most desires. You are the reflection of a reflection you embraced in the past.

BLESSING: Reflect on the past in hindsight, but be sure to focus more on the present in plain view.

YOUR MOTIVATION

LESSON ON HECTIC DAYS

Days are chances angels give us to make peace with ourselves. When we take this time for granted it results in hectic days. Now you may appreciate each day you awake, but what about each moment that goes into the day? What about investing in relationships, family, careers or self? The less you invest the more hectic your day will be. The more you lack appreciation for each moment no matter the circumstance, the more stress you will have.

BLESSING: When times get rough remember that sandpaper makes all things smooth.

YOUR MOTIVATION

LESSON ON LOSING LOVED ONES

This is for those who have lost a friend or loved one before their time.

Hello Angel,

How are you in that place that we have so many names for? Are the clouds soft as we imagine them to be? I would love to tell you how everything is going down here but I know you have a better view. I wish you were here in the physical form so I could hug you again. There are so many days I had things to share with you but I realize GOD gave you another mission. I pray for and exercise my strength to keep your spirit around me. Things have changed and now I understand why. I see what your role in life was. Anyhow, I have to cut this letter short because I hear your voice saying "speak in your walk, don't walk in your speaking." I understand but I must also remember...it's the love that does it. Keep your wings wrapped around my spirit and I will keep your name alive. I celebrate your life. Love you always.

BLESSING: May your life heal from loss and understand that you gained a guardian angel.

YOUR MOTIVATION

_____

_____

_____

_____

_____

_____

_____

_____

_____

_____

_____

_____

_____

_____

_____

_____

_____

_____

_____

LESSON ON GETTING WHAT YOU DESERVE

Being single, married or just partners—you get what you deserve. People say phrases like, "What did I do to deserve this," or "I don't deserve you." Do you say these words in relationships? Why are you single but want to be married? Practice dating to understand what communication means. Are you in a relationship you feel isn't going anywhere? Are you frustrated? Well you deserve it because you are not being honest enough with yourself to leave. Do you sit up all night waiting on her when it makes you feel less of a man? You get what you deserve because you are not allowing yourself to be who you are supposed to be in your relationship...and the one you are in isn't for you.

Go get what you deserve. Nobody deserves less of a person if they are investing more.

BLESSING: Claim what you want in a person and don't settle until you receive 99% of it because no one is perfect.

YOUR MOTIVATION

LESSON ON QUIET STORMS

Storms come in all forms. They can come in the form of people, family, or friends. Storms can be at school, work, or even at home. There are so many storms that no human being can hide from them. I have experienced many storms in my life and I must say that the most powerful storm is the quiet storm. This is because you never know when it will hit you. It could be an accident while playing sports, an accident in a car; it could even be bills that show up when you have no money. Quiet storms are the only personal storms that determine your strength, test your faith and help you decide if you are doing what you're "supposed" to be doing in life. If you are experiencing a quiet storm as you read this just be still and figure out what isn't strong in your life and strengthen it. Those who are not experiencing the quiet storm—prepare for it now, so when it comes you will not be moved!

Blessing: Calm waters don't make great sailors.

YOUR MOTIVATION

RAHFEAL "INFINITE" GORDON

ABOUT THE AUTHOR

RATHER BE HATED FOR WHO HE IS THAN TO BE LOVED FOR WHO HE IS NOT

FROM NOTHING TO SOMETHING

FOREVER GRATEFUL

HUMBLE

SPIRTUAL

OVER ACHIEVER

BRILLIANT

MORE THAN HE WAS YESTERDAY

SUCCESSFUL

IDEAL

To book Rahfeal Gordon for speaking engagements, order books or to find out more information about him, please contact us at:
Rahfeal@gmail.com
(973)449-5607

"I STAND TO BE DIFFERENT BECAUSE IT IS THE ONLY WAY TO MAKE A DIFFERENCE."

Breinigsville, PA USA
09 December 2009

228919BV00004B/3/A

9 780981 480503